THE LITTLE BOOK FOR CAT M🐾MS

THE LITTLE BOOK FOR CAT MUMS

An Hachette UK Company
www.hachette.co.uk

Summersdale Publishers Ltd
Part of Octopus Publishing Group Limited
Carmelite House
50 Victoria Embankment
LONDON
EC4Y 0DZ
UK

www.summersdale.com

Printed and bound in China

ISBN: 978-1-80007-006-6

Substantial discounts on bulk quantities of Summersdale books are available to corporations, professional associations and other organizations. For details contact general enquiries: telephone: +44 (0) 1243 771107 or email: enquiries@summersdale.com.

THE LITTLE BOOK FOR CAT M🐾MS

TIPS, ACTIVITIES AND INSPIRATION
FOR THE ULTIMATE CAT LOVER

CHARLIE ELLIS

summersdale

❀ INTRODUCTION ❀

Cats are elegant and stylish, mysterious and unknowable, yet adorable and charming. And so are cat parents!

Cat mums are resilient – we keep loving our cats even when they ignore us. Cat mums are giving – we heap beds, toys and treats on our cats in the hope they'll like just one. Cat mums have a good sense of humour – how else would we laugh off the trail of destruction left by the little darlings?

This book celebrates everything cat mum. It is filled with top tips to help you care for your fur babies, quotes from fellow cat fans, wise words celebrating the highs and lows of cat worship, and games to keep you occupied in between bouts of staring lovingly into your fluffykin's eyes. Fill-in pages will help you document your little one's likes and dislikes and there's even the opportunity to create art of – and with – kitty.

Pick up your cat, curl up and enjoy!

❧ CAT DATA ❧

Cat parent... or cat secretary? We'd say executive assistant to the CEO (Cat ExtraOrdinaire). Record all the need-to-know information for keeping on top of your cat's schedule, business meetings, errands and more.

- **Name:** ....
- **Breed:** ....
- **Birth date:** ....
- **"Gotcha" date:** ....
- **Microchip details:** ....
- ~~**Name of sworn enemy**~~ **Veterinary practice:** .....
  ....
- **Medication and jabs due:** ....
- **Date last wormed:** ....
- **Prescription details (if applicable):** ....
  ....
- **Notes:** ....
  ....

Stay fresh

While cats may not be a fan of bathing in water, they do enjoy partaking of a glass of fresh water. Often, it's your glass of fresh water! To keep your cat's eyes on their own bowl, remember to change your cat's water regularly, and keep it clear of dust, food, fur and other cat debris. Some cats don't like their water to be situated too closely to their food for this reason. If your cat is slow to drink, try changing its water regularly and moving it away from its eating area.

Cat gadgets

Some cats prefer to drink from running water. Although they may want to lap from the tap, this arrangement goes against most rules of hygiene. And we'll say nothing of the cats that like to sip from the toilet! Indulge your fussy feline by purchasing a cat fountain; they not only save on water but avoid you having to clean up each time your cat takes a drink. They come equipped with a filter so you can be sure your cat is accessing clean water. Cheap to run, cat fountains burble away at cat height. Just remember to change the water and clean the fountain regularly!

 SMITTEN KITTENS

Received wisdom says that kittens sleep for roughly 20 hours a day, but experienced cat mums know that it's more likely that they'll cause chaos for 20 hours a day! You'll need to have all the essentials in place to make the first days of having your kitten as smooth as possible. Brace yourself with these top tips for new kitten parents.

Essentials

Before you bring your new cat home, make sure you're all stocked up with:

- **Kitten food**

- **Food bowl**

- **Water bowl**

- **Cat bed**

- **Litter tray**

- **Cat carrier**

- **Toys suitable for kittens – not too large or heavy**

- **Grooming brush**

Making space

Start small. Set up a single room with dry food, water, a litter tray and somewhere comfortable to sleep for your new kitten. Be sure to block off any small spaces they may crawl into and get stuck. Your new itty bitty kitty will need at least a week in this environment to grow in confidence and establish a territory, after which you can start to slowly open up the rest of the house to them.

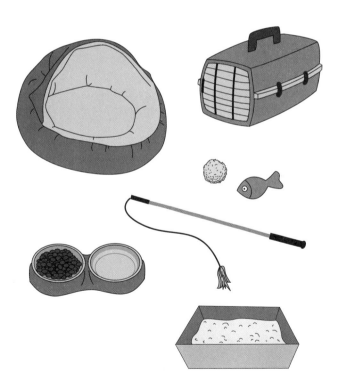

YOU HAD
ME AT "MEOW"

What's the name for a group of kittens?

A) A cuddle

B) A fluff

C) A litter

D) A purr

WHY I LOVE MY CAT:

My cat surprises me every day.

What greater gift than the love of a cat.

CHARLES DICKENS

Prepared puss

Be cautious when introducing kittens to the older cats of the house. Ensure each cat has their own clearly defined territory and keep them away from the new additions for the first week. Switch over cat toys or blankets so the kitties can get used to each other's scent. Before they meet for the first time, move the established cat to one room and let your new kitty explore your house for a short period of time.

New friends and enemies

When you do come to introduce the new furry frenemies, make sure you do so in a "neutral" spot and only for an hour at a time. Bring a couple of toys to give them something to do and show them they share common interests. Perhaps you can break the ice by leading a game of chase with a ribbon or teaser. Don't be worried if they aren't immediate feline friends; simply repeat the exercise over the course of several days (or as long as it takes) until all kitties seem comfortable with each other.

I CAN SAY WITH
SINCERITY THAT
I LOVE CATS;
FURTHERMORE I AM
GOING TO GIVE VERY
GOOD REASONS
WHY THOSE WHO
HATE THEM ARE
WRONG.

Emily Brontë

 POMPOM

If your cat is a lover of rags, tufts, balls and general destruction then you might want to make them a pompom to fulfil all their desires. You'll get bonus points if you make it out of an old t-shirt; it will smell like you, their dearly beloved – if slightly stupid – owner.

> **You will need:** old T-shirt or other soft material, scissors, old cardboard.

Method:

1. **Cut your old t-shirt into long strips, about a centimetre wide.**

2. **Cut two matching "C" shapes from the cardboard. The shapes should fit in the palm of your hand.**

3. **Sandwich a strip of material between the two shapes. The material should overhang either end of the "C" sandwich.**

4. Thread a strip of material through the centre of the "C" and wind it around the cardboard. Repeat with the strips of material until you have completely covered the "C" and can't fit any more through the centre.

5. Slide your scissors through the fabric and cut along the join of the two cardboard pieces. Pull the ends of the fabric sandwiched between the cardboard together and tie to secure the pompom shape. Cut around a centimetre away from the edge of the cardboard so the pompom material hides it.

6. Voila! A beautiful cat toy for your precious puss to play with – or ignore!

... you spend your hard-earned money on a beautiful cat bed, only for your cat to prefer a tatty cardboard box.

? Cats are all born with the same coloured eyes.

A) **True**

B) **False**

Cats choose us; we don't own them.

KRISTEN CAST

❀ ITTY BITTY KITTIES ❀

The cats listed below are among the smallest domestic breeds in the world. No wonder they've been lost in the wordsearch. See if you can find all of them.

```
T  F  A  G  H  I  A  O  S  P  H  Y  N  X  R
A  V  M  T  U  D  X  S  N  M  K  O  A  S  P
H  R  E  I  P  W  S  I  A  M  E  S  E  C  A
C  O  R  N  I  S  H  R  E  X  U  S  I  H  T
C  Z  I  M  T  D  O  L  K  R  E  C  K  I  A
D  H  C  T  W  Q  Z  N  C  N  O  P  D  M  E
E  C  A  U  A  S  R  P  I  U  M  G  K  A  S
V  R  N  D  F  L  M  L  N  I  Z  E  Q  L  D
O  C  C  H  Z  J  A  R  P  I  A  F  Y  A  N
N  P  U  E  X  B  O  M  B  A  Y  D  S  Y  R
R  V  R  C  G  J  T  Y  R  P  B  C  X  A  O
E  S  L  A  P  O  M  E  N  D  W  Q  U  N  J
X  N  O  M  U  N  C  H  K  I  N  K  M  P  R
G  A  I  X  Q  C  M  Y  P  D  S  A  C  O  R
P  D  K  A  M  I  S  I  N  G  A  P  U  R  A
```

AMERICAN CURL	CORNISH REX	SIAMESE
BALINESE	DEVON REX	SINGAPURA
BOMBAY	HIMALAYAN	SPHYNX
	MUNCHKIN	

17

HOME IS WHERE
MY CAT IS

How many breeds of cat are currently recognized by The International Cat Association?

A) 31   C) 71
B) 52   D) 94

You know you're a cat lover when...

... there's a subsection in your medical records titled "cat-related accidents".

When a man loves cats, I am his friend and comrade, without further introduction.

MARK TWAIN

Toothy problem

Brushing your cat's teeth is important for maintaining good dental health and is the best way to prevent gum disease, as well as other issues. Early signs that your cat is suffering from dental issues include trouble eating, excessive dribbling and foul breath. Your cat's breath may not be among your favourite scents but it should only smell meaty or fishy – not rotten. Check for inflamed gums – swelling or redness – by holding kitty's head firmly with one hand and lifting their upper lip.

Gnasty gnashers

If your cat is experiencing a build-up of plaque, try introducing more dry food into its diet. The abrasive kibbles will help clean your kitty's teeth. You can also buy cat chews to help keep plaque at bay. Still struggling with plaque and tartar build-up? Dental cat toys are covered in a fine mesh that acts as a sort of floss. As your kitty nips and chews at the toy, the mesh catches food flakes and build-up. Purr-fect!

✤ JOIN THE DOTS ✤

Follow the dots with the focus
- if not the vigour -
of your cat following a laser pointer.

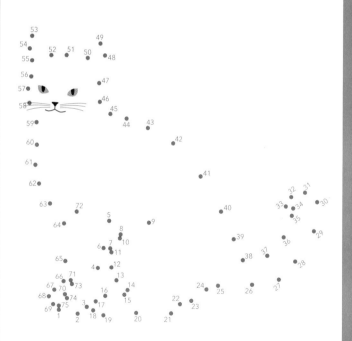

❧ ALL THAT LITTERS ❧

Ah, the glamorous world of cat ownership. Cleaning your cat's toilet isn't great fun for a variety of reasons, but having a clean and comfortable area for them to do their "business" is essential to a cat's well-being. Thankfully, there are a few things that you can do to improve your lot.

Eco-friendly

Eco-conscious cat owners might feel stressed by the options around litter disposal. Cat waste isn't suitable for composting and most litter isn't biodegradable. However, sawdust litter is available and provides a biodegradable, clean option, as do biodegradable litter bags.

Self-cleaning

Squeamish cat owners might want to consider splashing the cash on a self-cleaning model. Self-cleaning trays can sense when your cat has "been" and enact a range of cleaning methods, such as raking the waste out into a special compartment. You may still be required to empty out a compartment that holds the soiled waste as well as replenish the litter.

Monitoring

One of a cat's key indicators of health is in their toilet time. Health issues can manifest in the cat going outside the litter box. A range of snazzy gadgets are available that monitor anything from how often your cat goes, to their weight, which means you can be the first to know when something's out of sorts.

Business time

Cats are fussy about their litter – as they are about everything! But don't you prefer to "go" in comfort? The general rule of law is to have one litter box per cat plus one extra. This means your cat can enjoy a personal toilet and a clean spare for emergencies.

Undercover cat

Placement and size of litter tray is your cat's main concern – studies show that adult cats hold no preference for covered or uncovered litter trays. However, some cat mums might! Covered litter trays emit a little less odour and shield delicate human eyes from the nastiness our cats are capable of. Kittens can find litter tray doors a little challenging so you may need to unhook the door while your kitty adapts.

How many teeth does the average adult cat have?

A) 12   C) 24

B) 18   D) 30

Brush it off

Both longhair and shorthair cats need to be groomed regularly in order to remove dirt, grease and dead hair from their coat. Brushing also has other health benefits, such as stimulating blood circulation and maintaining skin health. Longhair cats can get themselves in quite the tangle and will need daily brushing to avoid discomfort. Some cats aren't fans of being brushed in certain areas – they are often very protective of their tummies. Persevere with your longhair cat as this can quickly develop into matted fur. On the other hand, shorthair cats' coats can suffer if overbrushed. As their coats are not as thick, their skin is not as protected from the bristles – this can cause skin irritation and thinning fur. Brushing your shorthair cat at least once a week should be sufficient.

Tangle-teaser

Don't reach for the scissors if you find a tangle. Firstly, try to tease the matted fur apart with your fingers. Once you've loosened the fur and reduced the matting, finish off the separation job with a comb. If the tangle is too large or stubborn, you may need to contact a professional to complete the job.

❧ TRIMMING THE TOESIES ❧

Too-sharp cat claws can hinder your kitty, causing them to get (adorably) stuck to chairs, carpets, blankets, themselves… the list goes on. This can distress your cat and your furniture.

Some cats reliably dull their claws themselves through scratching on posts and trees. Other cats… just don't bother. Here are a few tips for trimming your lazy kitty.

What to use

Buy special nail scissors at your local pet store or vets. Cat's claws are not like human nails – they contain the "quick", which includes blood vessels and nerves. Cut too high and your cat will bleed. The blade of cat nail scissors includes a little pincer feature, which you can use to staunch the flow if you accidently cut the quick.

Method:

1. Hold your cat firmly to your body, so that it feels secure.

2. Gently pinch your cat's paw between your thumb and forefinger, to push your cat's claws out of their retracted position.

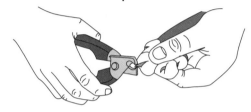

3. Line the scissors up to the apex of the curve of the nail, to avoid the quick.

4. Quickly and efficiently cut the nail and move on to the next.

5. Ideally, to cause your pet the least amount of stress, you would complete the grooming session in one go. However, cats are gonna cat. If either of you are getting agitated, walk away, let your cat (or yourself) calm down and return when you're both in a better mood.

What domestic breed of cat famously has no tail?

A) Maine Coon

B) Russian Blue

C) Manx

D) Bengal

You know you're a cat lover when...

... your new morning chorus is the chirruping of your cat and a close-up of their butt.

I love cats because I enjoy my home; and little by little they become its visible soul.

JEAN COCTEAU

Ear we go

Not every cat needs help cleaning their ears but frankly some bring shame to the name of cat. A clean and tidy ear should be pink or white, with no dark spots in or around the ear. Excessive dirt can build up in an ear in patches and even encroach onto the fur outside the ear. Your vet can clean your cat's ears during their yearly check-up but your pet may need a little extra attention in-between appointments.

Cotton on

To clean your cat's ears:

1. **Pick a time when they are relaxed, such as during or after a nap.**

2. **Dampen a cotton-wool ball.**

3. **Gently but swiftly swipe the ball around inside your cat's ear.**

4. **You may need to repeat the action to tackle stubborn spots.**

5. **Give your cat a treat for putting up with such undignified treatment.**

WHY I LOVE MY CAT:

They're an evil mastermind wrapped in a soft, fluffy hug.

Which country has the most cats per person?

A) UK

B) USA

C) Russia

D) New Zealand

**I have cats.
I'm obsessed with them.**

TAYLOR SWIFT

❀ ANAGRAM ❀

Your cat has got into your bookshelves and muddled up all the books containing cats. Some are literary classics, some are contemporary faves but all have their titles twisted round. Untangle these anagrams to rediscover your cat-themed literary library.

1. **Blowier hundredth picnic**

2. **Dalliance Rewind No**

3. **A Chat Teeth Hint**

4. **A Kaftan's Barest Fifty**

5. **A Grammarian That Rested**

6. **Act Huge Test**

7. **Master Peaty**

8. **Lanky Mini Silk**

9. **Aesthetic Din**

10. **Arc No Lie**

TOILET-ROLL TREAT TEASER

This craft is so easy, even your cat could make it. In fact, the aim of the game is that you create something your cat will then *undo*. This treat teaser lends another dimension to spoiling your cat. Kitty can only access their favourite treat once they've worked out the puzzle. The test gives them a little mental stimulation and play.

If that wasn't good enough, you need minimal resources to create this make. And, if you don't have a toilet-roll centre handy, you will eventually!

You will need: one toilet-roll centre, one or two crunchy cat treats.

Method:

1. Place one or two cat treats inside the cardboard centre of a toilet roll.

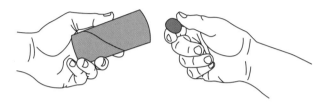

2. Press the ends of the toilet roll inwards so the ends form a crescent.

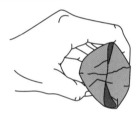

3. Rattle the treat teaser lightly to make sure the treats don't easily slip through the gaps at either end.

4. For an optional jazzy extra, you could draw a design on the cardboard. Your cat... will probably not notice. Or you could pierce a corner of the toy and tie a feather to it. Your cat is more likely to notice and appreciate this!

5. Hand it over and learn how keen your cat's problem-solving abilities are!

WHEN I'M WITH YOU I'M FELINE GOOD

What is the largest domestic breed of cat?

A) Norwegian Forest cat
B) Siamese
C) Serbian
D) Maine Coon

WHY I LOVE MY CAT:

My cat is as graceful as a ballerina... except when they're clumsy as a rhino.

The mathematical probability of a common cat doing exactly as it pleases is the one scientific absolute in the world.

LYNN M. OSBAND

TIDY-UP TIME

You and your cat have chased each other around your home, tangling their teaser around every available chair leg. Time to muster your best sudoku skills and **tidy up**!

I				T	U
			I		
	I				P
T				U	
		Y			
U	T				D

Keep it clean

Cats can be stressed by dirty environments (even though they provide plenty of the grub through fluff and dander). Where possible, keep your home clean of dirt and grime: vacuum and sweep regularly, with special attention to the areas around their litter trays and sleeping spots. Cats aren't generally stressed by a *messy* home – and often enjoy playing around piles of clutter – but take it from one cat parent to another, it's harder to keep a messy home clean.

Cat hack

The mightiest machine can struggle to pick up cat fluff, even if you've paid an absolute fortune for a specially designed pet vacuum. Instead, repurpose an old or cheap cat brush as a device to clean your soft furnishings and clothes. You'll be surprised how much you can lift with ten minutes and a cat brush. No brush and guests are due? Simply cut a length of sticky tape and wrap it around your hand, sticky side out. A few frantic pats and your furnishings will look like new.

You know you're a cat lover when...

... you can take or leave the holidays but your cat has their own Easter lunch, Halloween outfit and advent calendar.

Do not disturb

Do you enjoy people walking past your bed when you're trying to sleep? Neither does your cat! Try to set up your cat's bed in a quiet corner, away from busy thoroughfares such as hallways or hectic kitchens. You should also try to avoid cool or damp areas, or spaces near front or back doors. Not sure where to place it? Don't worry, your cat will tell you! Kitties aren't shy about establishing a favourite sleeping spot (or two). Once you've worked out your cat's favourite spot for snoozing you can move their cat bed and some of their favourite toys to the area. Don't be surprised if your kitty changes up their sleeping spot every three months or so. This is due to a wild animal instinct that urges them to rotate sleeping spots to stay safe.

Oh dear! Your cat has caught some mice. Better replace them with a more suitable toy. Change one letter at every rung until you've turned "MICE" into a "BALL". All the words in the ladder must be real words and be comprised of four letters.

MICE

BALL

WHY I LOVE MY CAT:

My cat thoughtfully brings me gifts (usually toys I gave them first).

Which breed of domestic cat is known for being hairless?

A) Siamese

B) Sphynx

C) Desert

D) Bengal

One cat just leads to another.

ERNEST HEMINGWAY

ROSES ARE RED,
VIOLETS ARE ACE,
I LOVE MY HUMAN,
SO I PUT MY BUTT
IN THEIR FACE

🐾 CAT GARDEN 🐾

Do you love your cat and your garden? What about growing some cat-friendly plants for you both to enjoy? Most cat-friendly plants can be grown in pots so are suitable for smaller gardens and balconies.

Catnip

Catnip is the quintessential cat treat. Cats react to fresh or dried catnip by flopping around, becoming more playful and generally being more of a goofball. Catnip is a mid-height leafy plant that can be grown from seed, and is good for borders, herb patches or pots. Catnip prefers full sun and well-drained soil.

Cat mint

Cats have a similar reaction to cat mint as they do catnip. Cat mint grows well in full sun or partial shade, in borders, herb patches or pots. Mid-height green leaves are joined in the summer by lavender-blue flowers.

Valerian

Valerian is often used in all-natural relaxing sprays for cats. It has a similarly relaxing effect when your cat chomps on the fresh leaves. Valerian has a large root system so if you are growing it in pots make sure they are large. These mid-height plants produce clusters of small white flowers and prefer full sun or partial shade.

Unplug your pet

Laser pointers can be a great way to work off your cat's energy without having to go to the trouble of jogging round the house yourself – you can even buy auto-rotating lasers for when you're away from the house. As long as you don't point the laser directly at your cat's eyes, they are harmless toys for your pet and it can be endlessly entertaining to watch. However, some animal behaviourists say that cats enjoy the act of catching and "killing" toys and may become frustrated with the laser dot eternally slipping through their paws.

Hide and bop

Cats' enjoyment of the laser pointer comes from mimicking hunting behaviour. You can up the deadly(ish) fun for your cat by adding an extra toy to their play. A tube or tent – whether home-made or store-bought – creates an environment they can hide in and pounce from. A good cat parent will pretend not to spot their super-sneaky-kitty, even when there's a whole backside and tail sticking out from the hidey hole.

DID YOU KNOW...

Hodge was a much-beloved cat belonging to English writer Samuel Johnson. He was a bit of a superstar in eighteenth-century literary London and his passing was even memorialized in Percival Stockdale's "An Elegy on the Death of Dr Johnson's Favourite Cat". By Stockdale's account, Hodge was a very mannerly cat indeed; "Who by his manner when caressed, Warmly his gratitude expressed; And never failed his thanks to purr, Whene'er he stroked his sable furr." Johnson's biographer Boswell wasn't quite so enamoured. He was, in his own words, "one of those who had an antipathy to a cat". We can't imagine that bothered Hodge too much, as he lived a life of luxury and regularly dined on oysters. A statue of Hodge now stands outside the house he once shared with Johnson.

WHY I LOVE MY CAT:

There's nothing sweeter than their tiny toe beans.

UPCYCLED CAT SCRATCHER

Is your cat's scratching post looking a little shabby? Has your cat taken its best years? You don't need to create waste by throwing it out and buying a new one. The rope wrapped around scratching posts and scratch pads is known as sisal rope. With some sisal rope and some basic crafting equipment you can fix and even improve the scratcher.

Most cat scratchers are available in a neutral beige but did all you colour-loving cat mamas know sisal rope is available in other colours? Oh yes, you can really customize your cat's scratching post to coordinate – or pleasingly clash – with your décor.

You will need: craft knife, sisal rope, hot glue gun, hot glue sticks, scissors.

Method:

1. Use the craft knife to cut away the remains of the rope surrounding the scratcher. Chip away any old glue left behind.

2. Starting at the base, wind the sisal rope tightly around the post. Dot hot glue just before you press the rope against the structure.

3. Hot glue cools and dries quickly, so you'll need to do a bit of juggling between dotting the glue and winding the rope.

4. Keep the rope tense against the structure as you wind it to ensure it adheres to the glue. Cut away any exposed dry glue.

5. When you reach the top of the structure, snip away the excess rope.

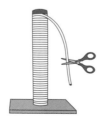

In *Alice's Adventures in Wonderland*, Alice encounters the:

A) **Cheltenham Cat**
B) **Chattersley Cat**
C) **Cheshire Cat**
D) **Cornwall Cat**

You know you're a cat lover when...

... you've mastered cat-buckaroo — you know the exact number of strokes your cat will tolerate before communicating with their claws.

The cat is an ancient, inviolable animal.

MIKHAIL BULGAKOV

Nice to meat you

Cats are obligate carnivores. This means, while they're not averse to a spot of egg, their diet must contain meat in some form. If sharing your plate with your kitty, avoid prepared meats that may contain too much salt, or worse, a spice that is toxic to them, such as garlic. The same rule goes for egg. Avoid serving raw egg to your kitty, but a little unseasoned cooked egg is fine. This treat is high in fat so avoid giving them too much, or treating them too often. If your cat has been particularly good, then you could prepare them their own treat by grilling - with little or no oil - a small amount of chicken. Chop finely to serve.

🐾 CAT FAVOURITES 🐾

One of the best recommendations for being responsible for your cat's welfare is to learn their usual behaviour so that you know when they're acting unusually. There is no one-size-fits-all rule for cat behaviour, so get to know your cat's little faves and learn what makes them purr!

- **Favourite sleeping spots:** ....

- **Favourite toys:** ....

- **Favourite food brand and flavour:** ....

- **Tastiest treat:** ....

- **My cat is a lover/fighter/eater/sleeper (delete any that don't apply)**

- **What noise does my cat make when they're happy?** ....

- **What noise does my cat make when they're annoyed?** ....

- **What kind of trouble does my cat enjoy?** ....

DID YOU KNOW...

Ever wondered what it means when your cat "chirrups" or "trills" at you? These are affectionate vocalizations that cats make to their kittens. In fact, cats don't usually make noises to other adult cats. Most cats only vocalize when they are kittens or when communicating with kittens. Or with you – their lovable but strange hairless cat baby. We're not sure why cats continue to talk to humans long after they've stopped mewing at their fellow cats. Perhaps they think we need all the help we can get!

Grumpy cat

Chirrups are good, so are grumbles and groans bad? Don't panic if your cat starts groaning in their sleep or if they're getting comfortable. They're likely not in pain – cats present discomfort in other ways – but just dreaming. Cats are old souls really, so is it any surprise that they should vocalize like Grandma sitting down after a hard day of spoiling you?

Dear diary

When you're not your cat's chef, maid, entertainment and therapist, you also need to be their secretary. Cats need yearly vaccinations and regular worm and flea treatments. Some vets provide a reminder service. If your vet doesn't, or if you want to be sure your cat keeps to its health-preserving schedule, set aside some time to get organized and enter a year's worth of dates in your diary. Set up your electronic device to send you reminders to book your cat's vaccinations and order the worm and flea treatments.

DID YOU KNOW...

According to an apocryphal story, Sir Isaac Newton was often disturbed in his experiments by his cat begging to be let in. He allegedly invented the first cat flap to ensure his beloved kitty could go her own way without disturbing him. He cut a hole in the door and covered it with black velvet. While this tale is uncorroborated, it's worth repeating on the strength of the cat's name alone... Spithead.

☙ TOY TANTRUM ☙

Your cat has scattered its toys everywhere and is now complaining to you that it's got nothing to play with. Look for these words in the wordsearch and highlight them when you find them.

```
F D H E A P O I N T E R N B M
R T G H A W C X S A W O Y I T
V X U G S B M O U S E L S S E
E S C N X N T I A Q W K O O A
L Y A R N A C E N T R P J H S
A P L H F E T J N C G H I A E
P B I N H W L J R N P O M Z R
U J A G V Y M F I P R D F S B
Y E N L P J C H B R S K T O A
B T R W L G C H B C T P I K M
R V T B N T A U O N R L K D S
A T P C A X R W N M I U F I C
D G H R J A W O X E N P M G L
G F C A D E C D A N G L E R A
P S K E G H C J A S K P E Q X
```

BALL   POINTER   TUNNEL

DANGLER   SCRATCHING   RIBBON
                        POST

MOUSE   STRING   YARN

                     TEASER

53

MY CAT IS THE CUTEST EVIL MASTERMIND I KNOW

The V-E-T

Cats are many things – often contradictory – but when it comes to the V-E-T they're not dumb. They know once the cat carrier comes out they're going in, and they're not happy about it! Greedier cats can be lured into the cat carrier by a Hansel-and-Gretel-style trail of treats leading to the back of the box. Other cats can be bamboozled by being quickly scooped and deposited in the carrier (keeping the carrier out of sight until the last minute can help). For more nervous cats, using pheromone spray on the inside of the carrier can help them feel calm and settled.

The V-E-T part T-W-O

De-stress your cat during a trip to the V-E-T by lining their cat carrier with something that smells familiar. This could be their favourite blanket or toy or an old t-shirt or hand towel of yours. Visiting the V-E-T takes your cat out of their normal comfort zone, so something that smells "theirs" can help to soothe them.

LIFE IS SHORT:
HUG YOUR CAT

✺ PAW PRINTS ✺

Couldn't you just stare at little beans - a cat's toes and paddy paws - all day? Why not put the time to good use and draw your cat's paws on this page? If you are particularly brave of heart or chilled of cat, you could even press your cat's paw to an ink pad and press it here.

How fast can a
domestic cat run?

A) 10 mph

B) 20 mph

C) 30 mph

D) 40 mph

WHY I LOVE MY CAT:

I can't resist
those big eyes.

When addressed, a gentleman
cat does not move a muscle. He
looks as if he hasn't heard.

MAY SARTON

... you've learned to identify your cat's toys by the particular pain they cause when you step on them.

DID YOU KNOW...

Maneki-Neko – literally translated as the beckoning cat – is a cat figurine thought to bring luck to its owner. Often portrayed seated with one raised paw that moves in a beckoning gesture, these figurines are also known in the western world as "lucky cats". The figurines are thought to originate in Japan in either Tokyo or Kyoto. The practice of keeping a Maneki-Neko spread in popularity throughout Chinese and Vietnamese communities and these lucky cats can now be found around the world. They certainly brought singer Netta luck when she performed her song "Toy" at the Eurovision Song Contest in front of a wall of Maneki-Neko, bagging Israel the 2018 win.

DID YOU KNOW...

Despite your cat's pretensions, the domestic cat's closest wild relative isn't a tiger. Nor a lion. Nope, not a panther. Sorry, kitty, not a jaguar either. The domestic cat's (Felis catus) closest relative is more like the tiny-but-mighty African wildcat (Felis silvestris lybica) or Scottish wildcat (Felis silvestris grampia). The exact date for cat domestication isn't known but it is thought to be around 7500 BCE, with African wildcats being the first breed to take up space in our hearts and homes.

WHY I LOVE MY CAT:

A tiny weight on my lap can lift a large weight in my soul.

For the birds

Sadly, our beloved cats are mad annihilators of the natural world. Now, especially, the eco-system is very fragile and cats can be an unfortunate tipping point. Cat bells drastically reduce the amount of prey caught. If your cat is a collared, outside cat, then consider adding a bell to help out your feathered friends. Cats rely on their silence to sneak up on birds, so a bell can help warn their would-be prey.

Holistic solutions

Some animal advocates recommend that cats do not wear collars. If you're uncomfortable with collars but want to reduce your cat's impact on the environment, then you could try adjusting your outside space. Opt for a freestanding bird feeder that will topple if your cat climbs it, and avoid feeders hung from trees and bushes. Birds are most active at dusk and dawn so avoid letting your cat out at that time, and keep an eye out for your cat on the prowl. A shouted warning can startle away unsuspecting birds before they become victims.

☙ CAT LOLLIPOPS ☙

What comes next may shock and alarm you but – and we can't stress this enough – this is a treat for your cat, not you. That's right, frozen cat lollipops. A touch of tuna brine, a meaty treat stick and a few hours in the freezer and you have a delicious summertime treat… if you're a cat. The lollipops are primarily toys but they should help your cat keep cool in the heat through contact.

You will need: one tin tuna, jug, 350 ml water, ice cube tray, cat treat sticks.

Method:

1. **Drain the tuna brine into a jug. You won't be using the tuna in this treat so you can store it in the fridge for later or donate some to a good (feline) home.**

2. Mix tuna brine and water and pour into ice cube tray.

3. Place in freezer.

4. Wait until the ice cubes have started to freeze – the time will depend on your freezer.

5. Insert single cat treat stick in each ice cube and return to freezer.

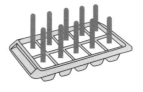

6. Once frozen, serve a lollipop to your cat! These treats are rich and too much tuna brine can upset your cat's tummy, so serve sparingly.

7. Voila! A beautiful cat toy for your precious puss to play with.

Boo!

No doubt your cat is a perfect angel. But if they were to be naughty, try making a loud noise such as clapping or banging, to startle them. A common suggestion is to spray water but one can't carry a water bottle around at all times. The idea is to stop the forbidden behaviour and break their routine. They might keep trying but they'll get frustrated with being unable to complete their naughty actions and eventually stop. But – and it's a big fluffy but – cats love to exploit loopholes. You've got to consistently discipline them, or else they'll learn they can sometimes get away with it if they're sneaky enough.

Care and attention

As a cat mother you deserve some love and care too! Although your cat is often only communicating or playing when they nip or scratch you, they can cause more harm than intended. This is because their teeth and claws can contain large amounts of bacteria. Always wash your cat-inflicted wounds with soap and hot water to avoid them becoming infected, and remember not to discipline your cat for simply communicating with you.

You know you're a cat lover when...

... one of your arms is your cat's deadly foe, who they are honour-bound to attack whenever they meet.

Time out

Despite their pretence otherwise, cats are great at learning a routine and being disciplined. If you're struggling with naughty behaviours and loud noises like clapping or spraying water near them isn't working, try the classic technique of putting them in "time out". When they're acting up, physically remove them from the situation and gently close them in a different space with no distractions such as toys or treats. Leave them in there for around 15 minutes to calm down. They'll learn that they don't earn any attention from their naughty behaviour and that their attempts to misbehave will always be thwarted. They should return with a new attitude and over time you should see a more chilled temperament in your kitty.

THE ONLY THING BETTER THAN A CAT IS TWO CATS

Milking it

Contrary to popular belief (probably spread by cats), cow milk is not a very healthy choice for cats. They may enjoy it but most cats are lactose intolerant and it can cause tummy upsets. Cats don't need to consume milk as part of their diet but if you want to give them a treat, serve cat milk. Cat milk is a processed milk that contains significantly less lactose than cow milk, allowing your kitty to enjoy it pain-free. Cat milks are easiest to find online or from your local pet store.

Cat that got the cream

Lactose, which is found in milk, is found in all dairy products. This means that other "traditional" kitty treats such as cheese and cream can also hurt your cat. Cats aren't aware of their intolerance and will often do their level best to convince you they need to have a crumb of cheese or a lick of cream. With great cat-parent power comes great cat-parent responsibility. It's hard to say no to your cat, but do consider that there are plenty of healthy alternative cat treats available that your kitty will love just as much.

❀ CAT NOPE ❀

Cats love sticking their little noses where they don't belong. Some cats in particular seem to relish gobbling up all sorts of edible – and non-edible – items. Oh, they might be poisonous to cats? *Cat shrugs.* That's your problem. Here are some commonly found items that are particularly toxic to cats.

Food

Anything from the allium family is a big no-no for cats. This includes kitchen staples such as garlic, chives and onion. If your pet is a bit of a walking trashcat and can't resist nibbling at whatever's on the floor, be particularly careful when cooking with these ingredients. Clean your worktop and floor after using and don't leave the foodstuffs exposed. Chocolate is also toxic (as it is for many pets) and they should also avoid caffeine, commonly found in tea and coffee.

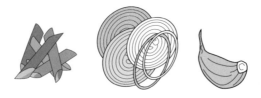

Plants

While some cats are floor vacuums, others are plant botherers. There are several common garden or pot plants that are toxic or deadly to cats. If you have a foliage-mad feline, keep them away from aloe vera, hyacinths, poinsettia and tulips. Lilies belong to the same allium family as garlic and onions: complicating matters, they are heavy pollen producers, which may drop on to your cat's coat or food, only for your cat to mistakenly lick at it.

You know you're a cat lover when...

... you've accepted that you don't deserve privacy. If your cat wants to watch you in the bathroom, that's their prerogative.

What is the smallest breed of cat?

A) Russian Blue

B) Rusty-spotted cat

C) Sphynx

D) Scottish wildcat

The cat is, above all things, a dramatist.

MARGARET BENSON

DID YOU KNOW...

Felix the Cat was Hollywood's first real cartoon superstar. Making his debut in 1919, the distinctive black and white cartoon featured in a "short" for Paramount Pictures. "Shorts" were short films which were screened before the main feature. In Felix's first picture, Feline Follies, he falls for the charms of pretty Miss Kitty White. He has since featured in several shorts, TV episodes and feature films. Felix celebrated his 100th birthday in 2019 by securing several brand deals, including a limited edition Sketchers collection.

Do cats dream of electric mice?

Although there is no definitive proof that cats can dream - they can't tell us after all - they do exhibit similar signs to dreaming humans. When humans dream they emit the same brainwaves as when they are awake and performing tasks - and this is the same for cats too. We can't know for sure what they are dreaming about but it's probably warm fluffy hugs (or total subjugation of the human race).

On average, how many hours a day does a domestic cat sleep?

A) 4-8 hours

B) 10-14 hours

C) 16-20 hours

D) 20-24 hours

You know you're a cat lover when...

... you have enough album material to release *Songs I Sing to My Cat Vol. I and II.*

WHY I LOVE MY CAT:

They have the dignity of royalty and the behaviour of a court jester.

RIDDLE

In Greek mythology, the Sphinx – a creature with a cat's body and woman's head – asked this of Oedipus:

**What goes on
four feet in the morning,
two feet at noon, and
three feet in the evening?**

I LOVE TO BE LAZY WITH YOU

DID YOU KNOW...

Cardinal Richelieu, a serious power player in France's history and legendary cat parent, was immortalized as an ultimate baddy in Alexander Dumas' *Three Musketeers*. Richelieu was indeed a schemer and powerful figure in the seventeenth-century French court, as portrayed in the novels. However, Dumas sadly left out Richelieu's passionate love of cats. He even built a cattery to house his host of kitties, comprised mainly of Angora and Persian cats. Among his 14 cats were Ludovic le Cruel (a prolific rat catcher), Cash on the Nail, Pyrame, Thisbe, Wig and Gazette. Pyrame and Thisbe were named after the poet Ovid's famous lovers.

You know you're a cat lover when...

... serving your cat's food five minutes late is considered a grave mistake. Serving it five minutes early is taken as the new deadline.

It's OK not to be OK

Your vet will tell you what signs to look out for with a newly spayed or neutered cat. If you spot any behaviour or signs of illness that match these signs, don't hesitate to contact your vet for advice – it may be that they need to be examined once more. However, not every sign of sadness is something to be concerned about – an operation takes a toll and your cat will undoubtedly need some downtime afterward! Your cat might well be a bit mopey and be uninterested in interaction. They may also be off their food for up to 24 hours.

Switch the litter

Vets recommend that you switch your cat's litter to torn tissue or similar during their recovery period after being spayed or neutered. This helps your cat avoid an infection risk from the clay or clumping litter. Your cat may be a bit suspicious but when they've got to go, they've got to go!

WHY I LOVE MY CAT:

We share our own special language.

How many whiskers does the average cat have on each cheek?

A) 6
B) 12
C) 18
D) 24

Cats can be very funny, and have the oddest ways of showing they're glad to see you.

W. H. AUDEN

❁ CATNIP TREE TRUNK ❁

This is an easy way to transform a delivery box into a great toy for your cat. The catnip adds another point of stimulation but cats who like scratching toys will enjoy it regardless.

> **You will need:** one or more large cardboard boxes, scissors or a craft knife, scotch tape, brown card (optional), catnip (available from most good pet stores).

Method:

1. Break down the cardboard box(es) and cut into long strips, roughly 2.5 cm (1 in.) thick.

2. Tightly roll one strip up and tape closed.

3. Roll a second strip around the first and tape closed. Repeat until your "trunk" grows to the circumference that you'd prefer. Ideally, it

should be large and heavy enough to provide a counterweight while your cat scratches and tussles with it.

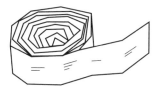

4. If you would like a polished look, decorate the outside with brown cardboard for a "tree trunk" effect.

5. Sprinkle catnip over the top of the trunk. It will fall into the gaps of the cardboard, enticing your cat to scratch and play with it.

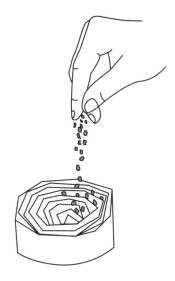

You know you're a cat lover when...

... you have three voices – your normal voice, your "speaking to customer service" voice and a "talking to my cat" voice.

DID YOU KNOW...

Who has two (or more) thumbs and loves fish? Polydactyl cats! While most cats have five toes on their fore paws and four on their hind paws, due to a congenital abnormality polydactyl cats have additional digits. This can give some cats the appearance of having thumbs! Ernest Hemingway famously owned a bevy of polydactyl cats. He was given a white six-toed cat named Snow White by a ship's captain. Hemingway's Key West, Florida, home is now part museum and part home to over 40 cats. Many of them are polydactyl and some are descended from Snow White. Hemingway owned hosts of cats in his lifetime, referring to them as his "purr factories". He often named his cats flamboyantly, including Princess Six-Toes, Feather Puss, Clark Gable, Uncle Wolfer and Furhouse.

Cat of the road

Cat backpacks are specially designed carriers for your cat. They are ventilated and spacious enough for your cat to sit comfortably. But will your cat be a fan? Well… it's up to them. The average cat feels most comfortable in their own territory: a space they are familiar with and that smells like them. They are likely to find being transported to a noisy, unfamiliar space unsettling (a little like a trip to the V-E-T). However, who has ever met an average cat?! Some cats do have a sense of adventure and, once they get used to the unusual circumstances, may enjoy nosing at the world. As an expert on your cat's personality, you're the best person to judge whether they would enjoy a cat backpack.

Angels with dirty paws

Does your cat love outdoor adventures but isn't so keen on cleaning their paws? If you're worried about puss picking up a paw infection – or simply sick of cleaning up after them – try giving them a paw polish. Hold your cat firmly against your body with one arm and, with the other, gently and swiftly wipe their paws with a damp cloth.

CROSSWORD

Test your knowledge of cat breeds with this crossword. Fill the crossword grid with the answers to the clues.

Across

1. This chatty catty shares its name with a tiger (6)
2. A type of cat, also a rug (7)
3. Just like everything else in America, this one is bigger (5, 4)
4. This dinky cat is named after its distinctive ears, Scottish ___ (4)

Down

1. These West Country cats are practically royalty, the Cornish and Devon ___ (3)
2. This breed of cat featured in Disney's Lady and the Tramp (7)
3. Densely furred shorthair, the ___ Blue (7)
4. You might find this cat in a child's playroom (7)

WHY I LOVE MY CAT:

They're my favourite photography subject.

A domestic cat whose coat consists of patches of different coloured fur is usually known as a:

A) Snakeskin cat

B) Tortoiseshell cat

C) Patchwork cat

D) Cowhide cat

> If I'm taking a walk and I see a cat, I'm happy.
>
> HARUKI MURAKAMI

Cat doctor

Cats run into many adventures and can sustain minor cuts and bruises along the way. If your cat has a small injury that doesn't seem to be causing them pain, you may be able to tend it at home. Clean the wound twice a day with a saline mix – create the mix by stirring 1 tsp of salt in boiled water, cool to lukewarm and apply with a cotton swab. Repeat until the wound has scabbed over. Keep an eye on the wound and if it starts exhibiting signs of infection, such as redness, swelling or oozing, contact the vet.

DID YOU KNOW...

Japanese author Murakami is famously fond of including cats in his fiction. This love of cats extends to his personal life. Before starting his career as a writer he owned a jazz club called "Peter Cat", named after a former pet. It was a success, and when the club moved locations in 1977 Murakami decked it out in plenty of cat paraphernalia. Visitors to the club would find cat coasters, photos and figurines. It was during this period that Murakami would write his first novel, *Hear the Wind Sing*. Beloved pet cats include Butch, Sundance, Mackerel, Muse, Black and Scotty.

❀ HAPPY CATTY ❀

Cats aren't the chattiest pets out there but they might be communicating with you more than you think. Kitties do a lot of their talking with their body language and behaviour. If you're wondering what's in your cat's heart, check out these helpful tips.

Body language

Ears and tail are the two biggest indicators of your cat's mood. Your happy catty will have upright ears and an upright or low (but relatively unmoving) tail. An upright tail should be curved at the top, like the head of a question mark, and a low tail should be loose and relaxed. Their mouths will be closed, and their eyes will be at "normal" size or lazily half-closed.

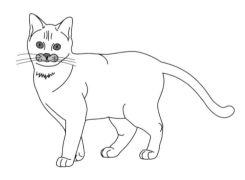

Noises

Of course, there is the famous purr! Cats do purr when they're happy but they can also purr to comfort themselves when stressed. If your cat's body language is saying "stress" (see page 104) then don't let a purr lull you into a false sense of security.

Behaviour

A purring, kneading cat is a happy fellow indeed. Look out for lolling, showing belly and general relaxation - this means your cat is comfortable and confident in your company. Crouching, pouncing and play-hunting is another good sign. Your cat is feeling playful and wants to interact with you.

YOU'RE THE PURR-FECT COMPANION

The only cat to have served as a leader of a political party is Catmando in the UK. Catmando led the Official Monster Raving Loony Party (OMRLP) with owner and co-leader Alan Howling "Laud" Hope between 1999 and 2002. Catmando was democratically elected to his position, tying for equal votes with Howling "Laud" Hope. After Catmando passed, the OMRLP proposed to pass a law that no other cat can be called "Catmando".

**The kitten, how she starts;
crouches, stretches,
paws and darts!**

WILLIAM WORDSWORTH

... you know the subtle difference between a "stroke me with your hands" and a "stroke me with your eyes" head bump.

Throwing shade

Your cat may be a sun-worshipper but they can overheat. Some light-skinned cats can even get sunburnt! Signs your cat is overheating include rapid breathing, a racing pulse and lethargy. In some extreme cases your cat may be unsteady on its feet or even vomit. Make sure your home and outside space is filled with shady spaces during the warmer seasons to ensure you have one cool cat. During very hot periods, your cat may become uncomfortably hot. You can purchase self-cooling cat mats – these gel-filled pads offer your pet a quick and easy way to get respite from the heat and return their body temperature to normal. You can also apply sunscreen to the exposed skin on your cat to avoid burns, but check the packaging reads "pet safe".

CATS CAN WORK OUT
MATHEMATICALLY THE
EXACT PLACE TO SIT
THAT WILL CAUSE MOST
INCONVENIENCE.

Pam Brown

❧ SOCK SWEATER ❧

Sock sweaters are cute! They can also be a less-intrusive way of preventing your cat from licking at wounds or infected areas. However, make a judgement call before you make this. They're great for kittens and small or medium cats, but if you have a chonky kitty you'll need a chonky sock.

> **You will need:** a large sock, scissors, marker pen.

Method:

1. **Cut the toe off the sock.**

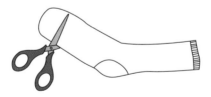

2. **Tuck the heel in and mark a semicircle along the edge of the tucked-in heel.**

3. Using the scissors, cut out the semicircle – this will create the front-leg holes!

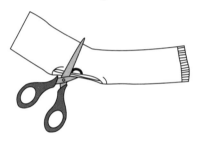

4. Voila! The sock sweater is ready to wear! But is your cat ready to wear it? Speed is of the essence when it comes to applying the sock to your cat. Be gentle but firm when putting their paws through the leg holes.

Remember that your cat is already wearing a thick fur coat, so a sock sweater should only be worn in colder months to avoid your kitty overheating and becoming uncomfortable!

Knowing your cat

The best way to understand when your cat is ill is to know their "normal". Be mindful when cuddling your cat and use the opportunity to give them a quick body scan. How does their fur feel (this may change depending on the season)? What is the temperature of their nose or paws?

Should my cat have...

A wet nose or dry nose? Cats largely have cool, wet noses. However, a dry, warm nose isn't a sign of illness in and of itself. Cats noses can warm up and dry out due to weather, their position in the house and a host of other reasons. However, keep an eye out for a warm dry nose with other symptoms.

Should my cat have...

Warm paws or cool paws? Cats' average temperatures are generally higher than humans' so their paws usually feel warm to the touch. However, cat paws can quickly cool if they walk on a cold or wet surface. If they warm right up again once they're dry and warm, then you have nothing to worry about!

WORD MAZE

Follow the famous cat owners to
get the cat out of the tree.

Ernest Hemingway	Catherine the Great	Elizabeth I	Edward VII
Winston Churchill	Isaac Newton	Elizabeth Barrett Browning	Audrey Hepburn
Karl Lagerfeld	Charlotte Brontë	Alexander the Great	Lord Byron
Florence Nightingale	Pablo Picasso	Doris Day	Salvador Dalí

NOTHING BUT CAT CUDDLES AND GOOD VIBES

❀ CAT PORTRAIT ❀

It's time to create a masterwork! Use this space to create art with your cat. You could sketch them at their stillest - a soft puddle of sleeping kitty - or snap a photo of them at their silliest - single leg in the air, hunched and startled - it's up to you.

Which Egyptian
goddess was half
woman, half cat?

A) Isis

B) Hathor

C) Bastet

D) Hesat

WHY I LOVE MY CAT:

They're a hot-water bottle
that doesn't need refilling.

There are no ordinary cats.

COLETTE

DID YOU KNOW...

In news that will surprise no experienced cat mum, scientists now suspect that cats domesticated themselves. Tracing the DNA and artistic portrayals of cats throughout history, scientists believe that they can only find signs of selective breeding from around the eighteenth century. It seems that wild cats followed the food, attracted to the higher population of mice and rats congregating around farming communities. There they discovered humans and decided to stick around, developing a symbiotic (some would say co-dependent) relationship. Sounds familiar. Certain traits, such as tabby stripes, started to crop up in cat DNA around the Middle Ages, but they weren't common enough to be associated with domestication until the eighteenth century.

Wiggle action

It would be useful to tell you why cats wiggle their bums a little when getting ready to pounce butt... the truth is, science just isn't sure. No one has ever conducted a study specifically around the science of cat pouncing (scientist cat mums, surely this is a field you need to enter). Cat experts suspect that it might add a little bit of momentum to their pounce or even be the result of a little dopamine being released into their system as they prepare to launch. In short, it's a happy wiggle!

❀ CATNIP FISH CRAFT ❀

Catnip toys are very easy to make and your cat will go wild for them. Clumsy-fingered cat mums fear not – this craft needs only a basic stitch.

> **You will need:** medium square of felt, pen, scissors, needle, thread, dried catnip, cotton wool (optional).

Method:

1. Draw a palm-sized fish shape on one side of the felt. Fold the felt in half and cut around the outline, resulting in two fish cut-outs.

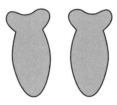

2. Sew the pieces together using blanket stitch, leaving around 2.5 cm (1 in.) open to insert stuffing. A blanket stitch always starts from the same direction. Insert the needle through both bits of fabric and pull the thread nearly all the

way through, leaving a small loop. Thread the needle through the loop and pull tight. Move your needle a stitch-length along and repeat. You'll create a looping knot around the edges of your fabric.

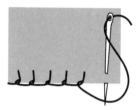

3. Insert dried catnip until the fish is full but not overflowing. This might be a lot of catnip! You can create a mix of cotton wool and catnip that will still tantalize your cat.

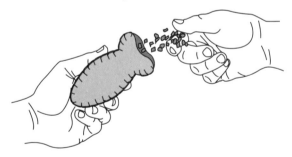

4. Sew the gap shut and knot the thread to finish.

5. Voila! Watch your cat go wild.

Destruct-o-cat

A little wear and tear is to be expected if you own a cat, but if your cat is really laying waste to your soft furnishings and other possessions, they could be suffering from under-stimulation. Up their quantity of toys or provide them with new ones, and invest time in playing with them too.

Midnight zoomies

By the same rule, cats who are particularly high-energy at night may not be sufficiently tired from the day's activities. Invest in some stimulating toys and playtime, especially just before bedtime.

DIY assault course

You don't need to purchase expensive toys to entertain your cat. Your environment can be lightly rearranged to create a temporary assault course or entertainment centre. Consider stacking cushions and draping blankets if your cat loves to hide or explore hidden areas. Of course, there is also the cat favourite – empty cardboard boxes. With enough boxes and a bit of ingenuity you can even create an amazing fort!

IN ANCIENT
TIMES CATS WERE
WORSHIPPED
AS GODS;
THEY HAVE NOT
FORGOTTEN THIS.

Terry Pratchett

☀ GRUMP-PUSS ☀

Knowing your cat is sad or angry might not make you feel very good, but it's the important first step in making them happy again. Most cats give a lot of clues that they're not thrilled with a situation before lashing out, so keep an eye out for the following signs.

Body language

Before your cat's tail starts puffing up it will likely be low and lashing. Look out for a rapidly moving, tense or heavy tail – your cat is working itself into a serious mood. Check out those ears too; flattened, flicked-back ears indicate a fed-up kitty.

Noises

Growling, hissing, spitting, yowling… an unhappy cat has a lot to say! Growls will start quite low in their chest and are usually in response to a behaviour they are unhappy with, such as a cuddle that's gone on too long. Hisses and spits usually say "stop it now!" A yowl is a truly miserable noise, indicating a pain response or perhaps warning another cat off their turf.

Behaviour

If your cat is hiding from you or sitting in a tense, crouched curl, they could be telling you they are unhappy. Cats can bite and swat for fun but they'll usually sheathe their claws and wrestle a little if they're playing. A short, sharp unsheathed swat or bite means "back off now".

DID YOU KNOW...

You'll have noticed the fine whiskers on your cat's face. But did you know cats also have whiskers on their forelegs? Oh yes. Known as "carpal whiskers", these help your cat determine whether their prey (or a "trapped toy") moves. Carpal whiskers pick up on movement when the prey is under their belly. When their prey makes a break for it, the cat senses the movement and can thwart their escape.

WHY I LOVE MY CAT:

They help me discover forgotten parts of my home – by hiding there.

Thither the whiskers!

Now and then you may find a whole whisker about the place. Don't worry, this is perfectly normal! Cats occasionally shed old whiskers as they grow new ones. If your cat experiences rapid whisker loss, it can be a sign of something more worrying. Cats lose whiskers as a result of an allergy, infection, stress or other ailments. As always, if you are concerned, consult with your vet.

Chatty catties

Some cat breeds are extremely vocal. They love to communicate with their pet humans! For example, Bengal cats are very chatty, so don't be alarmed if they have a lot to say. Siamese cats are also a vocal breed and can have long conversations with humans. These talkative cats will convey all their feelings, whether they are hungry, lonely, happy, mischievous, curious… they just won't stop. These chatty catties are a great breed for humans who like companionable cats.

Climbing catties

Cats also love climbing, so investing in a cat tree can be a good idea. Bengals in particular love being up high – and are real kings and queens of the castle once they get above you – so climbing apparatus is a real treat for them. However, a word of warning: this breed's love of adventure means precious objects that you've tidied up high for safety might not be as out of reach as you think.

A CAT GIVES
MYSTERY, CHARM,
SUGGESTION.

L. M. Montgomery

☙ JOIN THE DOTS ☙

Let's get ready, here we go,
join the dots, find this feline foe.

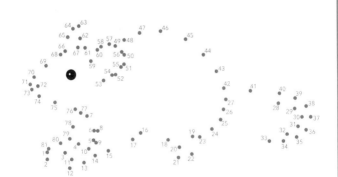

Sophisticated Sphynx

Sphynx cats were the first domesticated cat bred to be hairless. There are records of hairless cats going back to the Aztecs but the Sphynx was bred in the mid-1960s. They have slightly different needs to their fluffy feline pals. Their skin collects a build-up of oils, so they need weekly baths. Run tepid water and only use vet-recommended soaps.

Keep 'em warm

Sphynx cats can suffer a little from the cold. They're a good candidate for cat clothes such as a sock sweater (see page 92). However, if you do amass a little wardrobe for your Sphynx then you will need to remember to wash their clothes regularly. In the same way that the oils on their skin means they need a bath, the oils collect on their clothes. Another way to keep a hairless cat warm is to have plenty of blankets and maybe even a heated pad in the house.

ALL YOU NEED IS CATS

DID YOU KNOW...

Unsinkable Sam – or the cat formerly known as Oscar – was on board the German battleship *Bismark* when it was sunk. He survived, switching sides to British destroyer HMS *Cossack*, which was promptly torpedoed. Sam again survived and joined HMS *Ark Royal* as ship's cat. As you might guess, HMS *Ark Royal* was swiftly sunk but – good news – Sam survived. He decided to retire to a comfortable residence with the governor of Gibraltar.

Smelly cats

Substances that feel and smell nice to humans can be harmful to animals. In particular, essential oils, which can be a source of pleasure and well-being for humans, are toxic for cats. Do not apply essential oils to your cat's skin or fur and do not let them ingest any. Toxicity is reduced through inhalation, such as through a reed infuser, but could still be at dangerous levels for cats. Particularly toxic essential oils include peppermint, tea tree, citrus oils and pine.

WHY I LOVE MY CAT:

My cat will always judge me...
but never about the things
that matter.

What is the scientific
name for a domestic cat?

A) *Felis silvestris catus*

B) *Felix silvestris catus*

C) *Felix lionel catus*

D) *Felis silvestrix catux*

I have studied many
philosophers and many
cats. The wisdom of cats
is infinitely superior.

HIPPOLYTE TAINE

☙ MATCH X TO Y ☙

The word for "meow" is similar – but a little bit
different – the world round. Can you match
the international cats to their meow?

Minu the Maltese cat	*meong*
Hanh the Vietnamese cat	*mjaw*
Bygul the Icelandic cat	*mňau*
Chicha the Czech cat	*miyav*
Mimi the Indonesian cat	*mjá*
Leo the Spanish cat	*meow*
Pamuk the Turkish cat	*muallar*
Quruxsan the Somali cat	*meo*

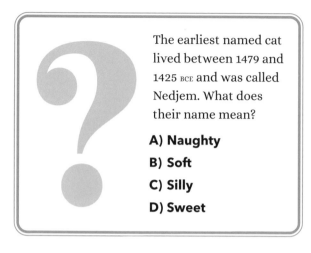

The earliest named cat lived between 1479 and 1425 BCE and was called Nedjem. What does their name mean?

A) Naughty

B) Soft

C) Silly

D) Sweet

Hamming it up

Your cat is right; it is allowed a ham-based treat! However, it should be more of an occasional indulgence and not a routine part of your cat's diet. Keeping ham as a rare and special treat can be a helpful way of getting a hesitant kitty to take medication. Pick ham that isn't drenched in herbs and spices, remembering that onions and garlic can be toxic to cats – they may upset your cat's tummy – and only feed them a third of a slice at a time. Stick to lean cuts to avoid high salt content. Due to its high content of fat and salt, bacon is a no-no for your kitty and should be avoided.

IT'S TOUGH-y TO BE FLUFFY

DID YOU KNOW...

You'll have heard that black cats are associated with several superstitions. Depending on which way they approach you – whether they are on land or sea, or if they have certain coat markings – they are considered lucky or unlucky. What you may not know is that, as a result of superstition, black cats are less likely to be adopted than their non-black feline counterparts. To try to rectify this, charities around the world have organized "National Black Cat Days" to celebrate our coal-black cat pals. If you're considering adding another kitty to your household, why not opt for a black cat?

What position did Stubbs the tabby cat hold in a small town in Alaska?

A) **Fireman**

B) **Mayor**

C) **Newspaper editor**

D) **Chief of police**

 CAT TEPEE

Is your cat a lover of dark and snuggly places? If so, they will love this DIY cat bed! At no extra effort to themselves, they can have their very own bespoke cat tepee. You may be able to use items found in your home, depending on your stock of bamboo poles!

> **You will need:** five 90 cm (36 in.) bamboo poles, 90 cm (36 in.) heavy-duty twine, one cotton scarf or blanket (at least 120 cm x 150 cm), five safety pins

Method:

1. Make an "X" with two poles on one side, and one on the other. The crossing point should be very high up on the poles, with only a few inches on the poles after the crossing point.

2. Tie a figure 8 knot around the crossed poles.

3. Stand the poles upright and gently spread them so they create a freestanding tripod. Lean in the remaining two poles to strengthen the shape and wrap the remaining twine around, knotting securely. This is your frame!

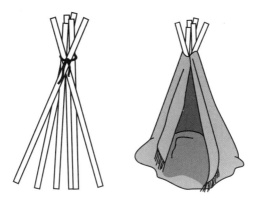

4. Lay the blanket or scarf out on the floor. Place the frame on one end and wrap the blanket or scarf up and around the frame.

5. Secure the material to the twine with safety pins, reserving one pin to fasten the material together at the top of the frame.

CAT!...
SLEEKY FLATTERER,
SPITFIRE CHATTERER.

Eleanor Farjeon

DID YOU KNOW...

Before Andrew Lloyd Webber's show *Cats* hit the stage, other cat-themed acts achieved fame in the theatre. One American vaudeville act was known as Swain's Rats and Cats. Run by Charles Swain, it first made an appearance in 1910 as Swain's Rat and Cat Circus. According to a *Variety* report in 1920, "One of the feature tricks is a cat stepping over seven hurdles on top of each one a rat is reclining." These cats shared the stage with some of vaudeville's biggest stars, including the Marx Brothers and Fanny Brice.

What breed of cat is known as a symbol of good luck in their native country?

A) **Siamese**
B) **Norwegian Forest cat**
C) **Korat**
D) **British Shorthair**

EXERCISE

On the whole, cats prefer to live their best life - eating, napping, being adored - rather than exercising. However, cats do exercise (albeit in short bursts) and they need to do it regularly or else they risk developing health complications, just like humans. But how to encourage your lazy kitty?

Outside time

Nature is the ultimate playground for cats. Simply being outside more can encourage your cat to pounce, jump and climb. These actions are the essence of healthful exercise for your cat, so make sure your cat has easy access to the great outdoors or be willing to open and close doors for them frequently - just don't forget they're out there!

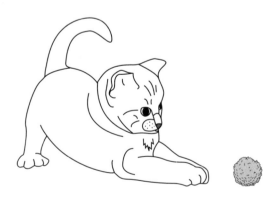

Toys

If your cat is an indoor cat then encourage them to play with toys. Don't worry – cats don't need to do lots of steps in order to be healthy. Short bursts of aerobic exercise such as chasing a ribbon or ball, or climbing a cat tower, will be good for your cat.

Change it up

Cats get bored with toys, just like we humans. Even if your cat prefers one type of play they may "go off" their usual toys. Try swapping out ribbon for string or a fluffy teaser, a normal ball for one that rattles, bounces or has a feather attached, or even introduce an automated cat toy that encourages them to chase and pounce.

MY FAVOURITE
TYPE OF PERSON
IS A CAT

DID YOU KNOW...

Salvador Dalí, the surrealist artist, was no stranger to a strange life. Among his pets was Babou, his pet ocelot. Ocelots are small wildcats with rounded ears and distinct leopard-like markings. They are certainly not a domesticated breed – although that didn't seem to bother Dalí, who would dress Babou in a studded collar and leash. Babou paced the halls of the most illustrious locations, including the St. Regis hotel in New York and aboard the luxury liner SS *France*. He also enjoyed the life of luxury when at home, reportedly having his own silk settee in front of the fire.

You know you're a cat lover when...

... you surprise friends, family and unsuspecting delivery drivers with conversations about your cat's toilet habits. It's all so interesting!

WORD LADDER

Oh no! You accidentally brought a strange dog home from the vets instead of your beloved cat. You'd better switch them back using this word ladder:

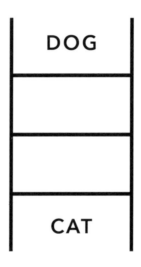

THEY SAY THE TEST OF [LITERARY PROWESS] IS WHETHER A MAN CAN WRITE AN INSCRIPTION. I SAY, "CAN HE NAME A KITTEN?"

Samuel Butler

DID YOU KNOW...

The first lady of fashion must be Choupette, designer Karl Lagerfeld's beloved white cat. She travelled the world with Lagerfeld and kept an entourage of her own, including two minders, a bodyguard, a doctor and a chef. She's even published her own book, *Choupette: The Private Life of a High-flying Fashion Cat*. Not bad for such a small mademoiselle.

So my cat's eaten something strange...

Cats will do anything they're not meant to! This includes eating things that they shouldn't. Any worried cat owner should consult their vet if they have concerns, but there are some rules you can adopt to help guide your pet healthcare. If your cat has eaten something non-edible such as a plant, ascertain how much they have consumed. If it is the merest nibble, observe their behaviour. If they don't present signs of sickness – such as an upset stomach – then they may be OK. However, if they have consumed something such as string or ribbon, consult with your vet straight away.

MY LOVE LANGUAGE IS CATS

Walkies

Have you considered a harness and leash for your cat? Cats don't need to walk long distances but there are plenty of reasons that you may like to use a leash when outside with them. A harness and leash can help you introduce a young cat to your outside area to familiarize them with their new territory but prevent them from running off. They can also be useful when re-introducing a cat to the outdoors after relocating.

Refuse to walkies

Most cats are not naturals with the harness or leash. Their initial reactions tend towards histrionics; acting as though their hind legs don't work, refusing to walk, lying down. This can be a common first reaction, so introduce the harness a little at a time. Put it on them for short periods - 15 minutes to start - and see if they get used to it. Some cats' love for the outside will soon overpower their dislike of the harness and they will start to acclimatize. For others, it's a permanent no!

Cats have fewer bones in their body than humans.

A) True
B) False

DID YOU KNOW...

Cats have been causing havoc since the start of human history, and there's proof! Archaeologists discovered a Roman tile dating back approximately 2,000 years. It is nearly perfect, aside from four small depressions – a cat print! Historians believe the naughty kitty skipped across the tile as it was drying. One fifteenth-century manuscript, found in Dubrovnik, contains a page of beautiful script. The only problem? It's marred by two small inky paw prints.

 CAT DIARY

Every moment spent with a cat is precious! That's why it's worth recording all the darling firsts you share together, as well as other special details. It doesn't matter whether your cat is a kitten making its first tottery pounces in the world, or an older cat with whom you're sharing firsts together. Fill in this little cat diary with all the dates and details.

- **Arrival date:** ....
- .... **is as big as a:** ....
- .... **'s fur is:** ....
- .... **'s eyes are:** ....
- **First favourite toy:** ....
- **First favourite hiding place:** ....
- **First naughty act:** ....
- **First time** .... **cuddled with me:** ....
- **First time** .... **jumped higher than themselves:** ....
- **First venturing to the great outdoors:** ....

Maine Coon top tips

Maine Coons have very thick coats indeed! In fact, they have three coats – two undercoats and one top layer known as a guard coat. That's a lot of hair! This gives them a very distinct appearance and keeps them warm during hard winters. It can also appear to be for the ignoble reason of covering your home in as much fur as possible! It's crucial for Maine Coon owners to remain on top of regular grooming, to help your pet and your furniture.

Grooming mitts

Get your mittens on your kitten! If your cat is decidedly not fond of being brushed – and you've tried both stiff and soft bristled brushes – consider a mitt. You can stroke your cat with these stubbly gloves, which come in a range of styles and materials, including a cotton glove with plastic or silicone nubbles for a very gentle experience. Your cat will get a massage and you'll get to shake loose any spare hair. Mitts can be purchased from your vet or local pet store.

I LOVE MY CAT
FROM THEIR
BEANS TO
THEIR BUTT

... you know not to sit in your cat's favourite, second-favourite, or back-up spot. You just sit on the floor, generally.

What is the term for a female cat?

A) Queen
B) Duchess
C) Lady
D) Marquess

Cats invented self-esteem.

ERMA BOMBECK

❀ CAT TOY SURGERY ❀

Cats can be hard on their toys; materials are soon ripped through, with stuffing pulled out and dispersed all over your floor. Instead of creating more waste by disposing of old cat teaser sticks, why not use them as a base for new toys.

> **You will need:** old cat teaser stick with hole, length of thin elastic cord, large needle, cat pompoms of varying sizes (see page 14).

Method:

1. Remove the destroyed toy from the stick. If the elastic or string is still in good shape, keep it and perhaps use it in this craft.

2. Cut the elastic cord to your desired length and thread it through the large needle.

3. Push the needle through the centre of one pompom and tie a knot after. If you are just using one pompom cut the cord here; if not rethread the needle and repeat with second pompom.

4. Thread the cord through the hole in the teaser and secure with several knots. If the stick has a big enough hole, you might like to add several strings of pompoms. Some cats will enjoy this pompom madness; others prefer a more elegant single string.

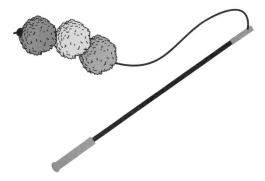

LOVE IS NEVER HAVING TO SAY YOU'RE SORRY

(ACCORDING TO MY CAT)

Cats have a dominant side, favouring their left or right paw. This is split by sex: male cats favour one side and females the other.

A) True

B) False

WHY I LOVE MY CAT:

They're a lapful of adoration.

There is no more intrepid explorer than a kitten.

JULES CHAMPFLEURY

❧ GOOD SCRITCHES ❧

Here's the definitive guide to how to stroke a cat without it getting grumpy with you. Maybe. It really depends on the cat. And even then they may change their mind…

Head

Pros: The head and neck can be a good place to stroke your cat. Try gentle massaging strokes on the crown of the head and along the cheeks. Some cats even like it when you stroke their little chins with one finger.

Cons: If this doesn't hit the spot for your cat, it's very close to their mouth , so be careful you don't get nipped!

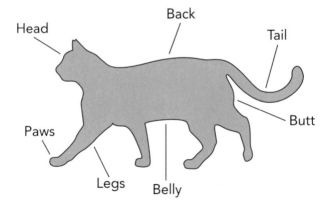

Back

Pros: A safe zone. You can't go too far wrong with long broad strokes with your palm along the length of the cat's back. Gain extra points for a little neck scritch.

Cons: A mostly guaranteed win but you lose points for creativity. Unlikely to find the spot that makes your cat swoon.

Legs and paws

Pros: You may personally enjoy stroking and squeezing your cat's itty paddy paws and darling toe beans.

Cons: Your cat will probably not personally enjoy this. It may accept it.

Belly

Pros: On the right cat, at the right time, this is a magic spot.

Cons: It's never the right cat or the right time. Danger ahead.

Tail and butt

Pros: A big scratch at the base of the tail is considered the good stuff. Your cat may kindly put its butt in your face to encourage you.

Cons: A tail stroke is too close to a tail pull for most.

THERE'S NO
SUCH THING AS
TOO MANY CATS

Cats can jump quite the distance! But how many times their length can they pounce?

A) **Three times**
B) **Four times**
C) **Five times**
D) **Six times**

WHY I LOVE MY CAT:

They inspire me to make my own way in the world... across the laptop, in front of the phone, over the table.

To respect the cat is the beginning of the aesthetic sense.

ERASMUS DARWIN

No visitors please

Cat flaps are great if you want your cat to be able to come and go at their leisure. However, sometimes the cat that comes in isn't the same one that went out. This territory invasion can upset your cat and cause fights, as well as give you a shock when a strange cat appears in your home! There are cat flaps available that only open in response to the microchip embedded in your cat – allowing them unrestricted travels and keeping your home free from unwelcome invaders. For the low-tech household, most cat flaps have a locking mechanism that will help you control who goes in and out of your home. Just remember to lock your cat in, not out!

The benefits of microchips

Cats are free wheelers. Cunning free wheelers who may wriggle out of their collar, leaving all identification behind! A microchip contains identifying information, including your contact details. This can be immensely helpful for charities and vets trying to return errant kitties to their homes. It takes seconds for a vet to microchip a kitty and is a process very unlikely to upset them, so is highly recommended.

☙ TIDY THE TOYS ☙

Oh dear, puss has got all their toys out
and not put ANY of them away. Locate all five
of the hidden toys before you can relax.

THEY'RE TOTALLY
PAW-SOME

Quick, release!

Cat collars have their plus points. You can ensure your cat has a bell to warn unsuspecting prey and a tag with home information. However, there are some risks involved. Collars can get caught and present a choking hazard. Most collars have a quick release, or breakaway, catch which means the catch will open when pressure is exerted. Retro-styled buckle collars do not have this mechanism so although they look good, do consider your cat's health when selecting these collars. The very slight downside of a quick-release collar is that some cats do regularly come home sans collar (you may suspect there is a pile of discarded collars out there somewhere). But really, a handful of lost collars is worth it!

Reflective collars

You may want to offer a little bit of extra protection to your cat when they go out at night. Reflective cat collars can increase your cat's night-time visibility, helping cars and cyclists avoid them without compromising on their overall comfort. These can provide peace of mind if your cat is a bit of a night owl.

Big booty cats

A healthy cat weight will depend on the cat's length, height and breed – there is no one-size-fits-all recommendation. Your vet can advise whether your cat is at a healthy weight during its yearly check-up. If your cat is not an ideal weight, they can also discuss your cat's eating regime and suggest some simple fixes, such as using a measuring cup or scales when pouring their food. In the meantime, you can monitor your cat with tactile checks – you should be able to feel their ribs under a slight fat covering and see the cat's waist when it is standing. Remember, cats are little accordions. They might look larger when curled up or sat in a squat or "loaf" shape.

You know you're a cat lover when...

... you're subtly trying to soft launch your cat's social media career. Smile for mummy!

Listen to your cat...

The care tips inside this book are all based on the behaviour of an average feline – but your cat is no average cat! All kitties are different; if your cat doesn't make a certain noise or isn't fond of a certain toy then that doesn't mean something is wrong with them. Cats have their own personalities, just like us humans. You know your kitty better than anyone else so will be fine-tuned to any unusual behaviour. All that matters, though, is that your cat's behaviour is consistent, and they are healthy and happy.

... and your vet

Having said that, always check with your vet if you are concerned about your cat's well-being. Your kitty's health and happiness should be top priority. Your vet can give you bespoke advice based on their expert knowledge and their familiarity with your cat. Many vets and insurance services also now run hotlines and FAQs, so they can help guide you through the smaller questions as you build your knowledge.

A CAT POURS HIS BODY ON THE FLOOR LIKE WATER. IT IS RESTFUL JUST TO SEE HIM.

William Lyon Phelps

✦ HIDDEN KITTEN ✦

Your cat is hiding in this wordsearch!
Can you see them?

```
R  Y  A  Z  E  V  B  J  D  H  E  I  L  P  Q
H  T  G  A  W  P  A  W  P  Q  N  Y  E  D  A
E  A  B  T  K  N  S  D  A  R  C  S  K  E  P
D  I  J  V  A  H  K  N  I  X  O  Q  U  D  L
L  L  N  U  X  B  P  J  D  N  N  Y  N  L  E
A  X  J  G  E  V  U  I  P  D  G  B  Z  E  G
P  H  Y  F  A  B  J  W  T  L  N  F  L  D  O
F  H  F  U  R  D  R  A  H  H  K  T  D  C  K
I  A  H  M  I  P  G  D  X  I  J  C  L  A  W
P  J  D  H  B  Y  I  L  P  D  S  B  T  E  W
M  J  G  U  Y  T  R  C  V  H  K  K  H  B  C
P  E  H  L  N  V  R  D  A  E  C  M  E  O  G
U  F  L  E  S  V  S  H  O  U  L  D  E  R  T
Y  E  A  F  R  S  C  G  X  E  R  P  L  N  G
B  M  H  G  D  S  R  H  A  O  Y  H  A  P  J
```

BELLY   FUR   SHOULDER
CLAW   LEG   TAIL
EAR   NOSE   WHISKER
               PAW

151

❀ OLDER CATS ❀

Though they may not be as small and squishy as tiny kitties, older cats can be fantastic pets and wonderful companions. As well as being less demanding in general, older cats tend to be more mellow and chilled, meaning a more peaceful household overall. Senior cats are the same floofer they ever were, just with a few extra things to watch out for. Here are a few simple tips for caring for your older gentlecat.

Diet

Cats generally drink less than they should, but once they become seniors they are even more prone to the side effects of dehydration, such as kidney disease. Make sure there are plenty of drinking stations around your home and to change your cat's water regularly. Feeding your cat wet food can also help keep it hydrated.

Health

Older cats are particularly susceptible to dental health issues. Keep an eye on your cat's dental health: check their teeth regularly if they'll allow it, monitor their weight and see how comfortable they are eating dry food and treats. Don't neglect the vet trips at this time as it's especially important your pet sees a professional.

Accessibility

Arthritic and less-mobile cats might not be able to reach their favourite spots as easily. Ensure your home is filled with cosy, private corners on the ground level where your cat can sleep and eat in comfort.

DO I CONTRADICT MYSELF? VERY WELL, THEN I CONTRADICT MYSELF, I AM LARGE, I CONTAIN MULTITUDES.

Walt Whitman

❀ CONCLUSION ❀

There is no evidence that Walt Whitman was talking about cats when he wrote those lines, but he might as well have been. And it's true – tiny as they are, cats are large. They do contain multitudes. And it's a true privilege to be the object of their particular brand of intense, mercurial, long-lasting love.

Although we tease our cats about their bad attitudes and pretend to each other that we are loathed by the furry recipients of our adoration, the truth is that it's a wonderful thing to be loved by a cat. Who hasn't enjoyed being woken up at 3 a.m. by a purring, kneading, inconveniently placed puss-cat, determined to convey the full might of their powerful – if weird – love?

All we can do is work to deserve that love (perhaps by showering them with DIY cat gifts from these pages) and continue giving them our best.

❧ ANSWERS ❧

p.11 What's the name for a group of kittens?
Answer: C) Litter

p.16 Cats are all born with the same coloured eyes.
Answer: A) True

p.17 Itty bitty kitties

p.19 How many breeds of cat are currently recognized by The International Cat Association?
Answer: C) 73

p.21 Join the dots

p.24 How many teeth does the average adult cat have?
Answer: D) 30

p.28 What domestic breed of cat famously has no tail?
Answer: C) Manx

p.30 Which country has the most cats per person?
Answer: C) Russia

p.31 Anagram
1. *The Wind-up Bird Chronicle*
2. *Alice in Wonderland*
3. *The Cat in the Hat*
4. *Breakfast at Tiffany's*
5. *The Master and Margarita*
6. *The Guest Cat*
7. *Pet Sematary*
8. *Slinky Malinki*
9. *The Cat Inside*
10. *Coraline*

p.35 What is the largest domestic breed of cat?
Answer: D) Maine Coon

p.36 Tidy-up time

I	Y	P	D	T	U
D	U	T	I	P	Y
Y	I	U	T	D	P
T	P	D	Y	U	I
P	D	Y	U	I	T
U	T	I	P	Y	D

p.39 Word ladder

MICE
MILE
MILL
BILL
BALL

p.40 Which breed of domestic cat is known for being hairless?
Answer: B) Sphynx

p.48 In *Alice's Adventures in Wonderland*, Alice encounters the:
Answer: C) Cheshire Cat

p.53 Toy tantrum

p.58 How fast can a domestic cat run?
Answer: C) 30 mph

p.70 What is the smallest breed of cat?
Answer: B) Rusty-spotted cat

p.72 On average, how many hours a day does a domestic cat sleep?
Answer: C) 16-20 hours

p.73 Riddle
Answer: A) human. A baby crawls (four feet), an adult walks (two feet) and an older person eventually walks with a stick (three feet).

p.77 How many whiskers does the average cat have on each cheek?
Answer: B) 12

p.82 Crossword

p.84 A domestic cat whose coat consists of patches of different coloured fur is usually known as a:
Answer: B) Tortoiseshell cat

p.95 Word maze

p.98 Which Egyptian goddess was half woman, half cat?
Answer: C) Bastet

p.109 Join the dots

p.113 What is the scientific name for a domestic cat?
Answer: A) Felis silvestris catus

p.114 Match X to Y

Minu the Maltese cat — meong
Hanh the Vietnamese cat — mjaw
Bygul the Icelandic cat — mñau
Chicha the Czech cat — miyav
Mimi the Indonesian cat — mjá
Leo the Spanish cat — meow
Pamuk the Turkish cat — muallar
Quruxsan the Somali cat — meo

p.115 The earliest named cat lived between 1479 and 1425 BCE and was called Nedjem. What does their name mean?
Answer: D) Sweet

p.117 What position did Stubbs the tabby cat hold in a small town in Alaska?
Answer: B) Mayor

p.121 What breed of cat is known as a symbol of good luck in their native country?
Answer: C) Korat

p.126 Word ladder

p.131 Cats have fewer bones in their body than humans.
Answer: B) False

p.135 What is the term for a female cat?
Answer: A) Queen

p.139 Cats have a dominant side, favouring their left or right paw. This is split by sex: male cats favour one side and females the other.
Answer: A) True

p.143 Cats can jump quite the distance! But how many times their length can they pounce?
Answer: D) Six times their length.

p.145 Tidy the toys

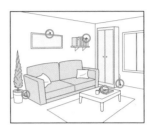

p.151 Hidden kitten

If you're interested in finding out more about our books, find us on Facebook at Summersdale Publishers, on Twitter at @Summersdale and on Instagram at @summersdalebooks

www.summersdale.com